AVALANCHE
AWARE

AVALANCHE AWARE

THE ESSENTIAL GUIDE TO AVALANCHE SAFETY

Second Edition

John Moynier

FALCON GUIDE®

GUILFORD, CONNECTICUT
HELENA, MONTANA
AN IMPRINT OF THE GLOBE PEQUOT PRESS

A FALCON GUIDE ®

Copyright © 1998 and 2006 Morris Book Publishing, LLC
Previously published by Falcon Publishing, Inc.

Falcon and FalconGuide are registered trademarks of Morris
Book Publishing, LLC.

Illustrations by Todd Telander

Library of Congress Cataloging-in-Publication Data is
available.
ISBN-13: 978-0-7627-3803-8
ISBN-10: 0-7627-3803-0

Manufactured in the United States of America
Second Edition/First Printing

This book is dedicated to Allan Bard, who passed away in a guiding accident in July 1997. Bardini was the epitome of a mountain guide; he was a mentor, sage, leader, and most of all, an inspiration to all of us who love the backcountry, especially in winter. He will be greatly missed.

Acknowledgments

I would like to thank the many fine people who helped with this project. First, I would like to thank Norm Wilson for the inspiration and guidance he has given me over the course of many years. I would also like to thank Allan Bard, David Beck, Peter Lev, Doug Robinson, Dan Whitmore, and Rick Wyatt for introducing me to the nuances of backcountry ski guiding and avalanche evaluation. Lastly, I would like to thank Steve Conger of the *Avalanche Review,* as well as Evelyn Lees, Tom Kimbrough, and Bruce Tremper of the USDAFS Avalanche Forecasting Center in Alta, Utah.

Contents

Preface

The dangerous lack of avalanche awareness by those who travel the mountains in winter often surprises me. Every year an average of about thirty people lose their lives in avalanche-related accidents that could have been easily avoided. Novices and an amazingly high percentage of expert skiers, snowboarders, mountaineers, and snowmobilers give little or no thought to the stability of the snowpack before committing to a slope, even though their lives depend on it. These folks play a dangerous game of "avalanche roulette" without even knowing how many chambers are loaded.

It is not my intent to scare people away from visiting the mountains in winter. On the contrary, by increasing awareness and understanding of avalanches, more people can safely enjoy a lifetime of winter fun in the mountains. In this book I have provided a practical approach to understanding avalanche danger.

Beyond this book, I encourage you to learn more about avalanches and the conditions that affect snowpack stability. The best way to do this is to take an avalanche course taught in the field by an avalanche professional.

Introduction

Most people who travel in the mountains in winter, no matter where they live, are exposed to avalanche danger. All it takes is snow, slope, and a trigger to make a slide. The trick is to recognize whether or not conditions are stable enough to allow safe travel.

When conditions are not clearly stable, we need to learn how to avoid being the trigger that causes a potentially fatal avalanche. Developing safe-travel skills, as well as self-rescue skills, is just as important as developing climbing, skiing, or snowmobile-handling skills.

Within the pages of this book are the essentials to understanding avalanches and also the most common circumstances that produce them. This book also explains the basic physical processes that occur within the snowpack and how they affect snowpack stability, as well as a variety of ways to test the snowpack for stability.

In addition, the text covers the basics of safe travel in avalanche terrain, including route selection and risk minimization. A list of proper equipment to carry for your own safety, avalanche survival tips, and rescue techniques for avalanche victims are provided. Information about increasing your avalanche awareness and the places to receive additional avalanche education are also included.

Learning about avalanches is only the first step in preparing for avalanche country. This book is, after all, just an introduction; unfortunately, training for avalanche country is not a science but rather an art learned from practice, experience, and patience. Much of determining avalanche hazard is a subjective evaluation of a variety of clues, some obvious, some more subtle. You can gain a lot of safe-travel knowledge by spending time in the mountains, but nature can also be a harsh teacher. If you plan to travel in avalanche terrain, it is important to learn at least the basics of avalanche hazard and to become more avalanche aware. It might save you from a potentially tragic situation.

Avalanche Basics

WHAT IS AN AVALANCHE?

An avalanche is an uncontrolled movement of snow. It can happen to a whole mountainside or only to the snow that fills a small side of a narrow gully. Avalanches occur in any area with significant snowfall and steep slopes. Unfortunately, this is often the best terrain for skiing, snowboarding, snowshoeing, mountaineering, and snowmobiling.

Avalanches are a natural phenomenon. They occur when the stress applied to the snowpack exceeds the amount of stress the snowpack is able to absorb. This happens either because of the heavy accumulation of new snow (excessive loading) or the progressive weakening of the snowpack (physical processes leading to crystal changes).

Avalanche Ingredients

- Steep terrain (slopes over thirty degrees)
- Smooth slopes

- Exposure to wind and sun
- Heavy snow, wind, or rain
- Rapid temperature change
- Prolonged periods of very cold or very warm temperatures
- Poor bonds between layers in the snowpack
- Weak layers in snowpack

WHAT IS AVALANCHE HAZARD?

Avalanche hazard is a threat to human life or property from potential avalanches. To evaluate avalanche hazard, it is necessary to estimate the stability of the snowpack on a given slope and the amount of stress that can be applied before it fails.

Stability of Snowpack

In addition to estimating the stability of the snowpack, try to determine what the danger or risk would be if the slope failed and produced an avalanche.

$$\text{Stability of Snowpack} = \frac{\text{Stress applied to snowpack}}{\text{Ability of snowpack to absorb stress}}$$

If an avalanche occurs in the backcountry with no one around, there is no hazard. An avalanche is only a hazard when a skier, hiker, or climber is in the way. Judging avalanche hazard is a matter of determining how close to a state of equilibrium the snowpack is and how much stress it may take to tip the scales.

WHO IS MOST AT RISK?

Winter hikers, mountaineers, snowshoers, snowmobilers, snowboarders, and skiers are the most obvious persons at risk. Generally, the more skilled you are at these sports, the more likely you are to seek out and spend time in potentially hazardous avalanche terrain and conditions. The average avalanche victim is a twenty-eight-year-old male, skilled at his winter sport but ignorant of basic avalanche awareness. Most avalanche victims trigger the slide that kills them by venturing into the starting, or "trigger," zone of the slide path.

HOW DOES AN AVALANCHE HAPPEN?

Avalanches occur when the external stresses on a snowpack exceed the internal strength of the snowpack to absorb them. Sometimes this is a slow process; other times it is a very rapid event. If stress is applied to the snowpack too quickly or is too great, the slope will become dangerously unstable and will often slide naturally.

The force or action that upsets the balance of the snowpack and sets the slope in motion is called a trigger. How big of a trigger it will take to get the snow

Figure 1. Typical avalanche path

to move depends on how close the snowpack is to the point of equilibrium. It may take an additional loading of new snow, the shock of a cornice collapsing on the slope, or simply the added weight of an unsuspecting skier or snowmobiler. The weakening of the snowpack through internal changes can also upset this balance, but more on that later.

Avalanche Triggers

- Weight of skier or climber
- Heavy, new snow
- Cornice (hardened crest of a ridge) collapse
- Earthquake
- Intense heat from the sun
- Rain
- Internal weakening of snowpack
- Rock fall
- Rapid warming or cooling

ARE THERE DIFFERENT KINDS OF AVALANCHES?

Avalanches are classified based on the cohesiveness (the tendency of the snow to stick together) of the snow as it begins to move, and they are defined as either loose-snow or slab. We usually think of an avalanche as being a massive wall of snow that decimates everything in its path. But even a seemingly harmless snowslide can knock a skier off her feet, depositing enough snow to bury her. An avalanche does not have to be very big to kill; many people have died in slides that were less than a foot deep and traveled less than 100 yards! A small slide may also be enough to throw a climber off her stance and over a cliff or into a crevasse.

Loose-snow Avalanches

Loose-snow avalanches (also known as "point-release" avalanches or "sluffs") begin with a small amount of

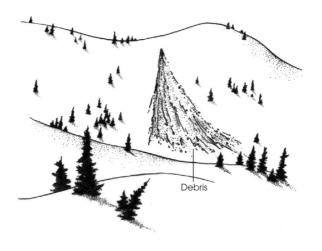

Debris

Figure 2. Loose-snow avalanche

snow and pick up more snow as they move down the slope, eventually leaving a fan-shaped track. These avalanches are often associated with dry, new snow accumulated without wind, but they can also involve wet snow, especially when a layer of snow becomes saturated due to very warm temperatures or rain. Most loose-snow avalanches are small, but larger slides are possible in wet snow conditions. Small, wet slides can also become the trigger for other, more dangerous, slab avalanches downslope. Figure 2 shows the elements of a typical loose-snow avalanche.

Slab Avalanches

Slabs form when a dense layer of snow is deposited on top of a weaker layer. If the weaker layer below collapses, the more cohesive layer (the slab) above will likely fail and begin moving as a unit. Slab avalanches can be very dense and hard or very soft, like new powder snow, depending on the cohesiveness of snow crystals within that layer. A small area of snow may start moving, or a whole hillside might move, depending on the size of the collapse, the steepness of the slope, or the slope configuration.

Slab avalanches are considered the greatest threat to winter travelers and are responsible for the majority of avalanche-related injuries and deaths. The chances of surviving a loose-snow avalanche are better than the chances of surviving a slab avalanche, primarily

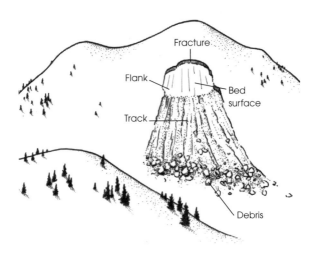

Figure 3. Slab avalanche

because of the large amount and force of cohesive snow moving all at once. Figure 3 shows a typical slab avalanche.

How Do Slabs Form?

Wind is a major factor in the formation of slabs because it can deposit loose snow into dense, cohesive layers, especially on downwind or leeward slopes. Strong winds erode snow on windward slopes and then redeposit it on the leeward slope. Because of the eddying nature of these winds as they slow, the snow crystals are frequently deposited in dense layers or slabs. Densification due to the effects of wind occurs as the snow crystals are tumbled against one another and the original stellar shape is broken. The wind deposits the snow on the leeward side of the feature (ridge, rock, etc.), and the broken crystals of snow can pack more closely together. The ability to recognize the leeward side of a land feature is important, especially for identifying where dangerous slabs may develop. Hence, it is important to determine wind direction during a storm.

Slabs are not only formed by wind. A number of other conditions can foster cohesion between snow crystals, including temperature and humidity. How well the slab bonds to the layer below and whether the supporting layer is weaker than the overlying layer are significant factors.

Slabs can form on any slope, but they are the biggest concern on thirty- to fifty-degree slopes. Studies of slab avalanches show that they most commonly occur on slopes close to thirty-eight degrees, which happens to be prime terrain for most winter sports. On slopes of more than fifty degrees, snow is likely to sluff off before it accumulates into a slab. However, very wet snow can even stick to vertical rock faces. On slopes of less than thirty degrees, an impressive amount of snow can accumulate, but the slopes are not usually steep enough to cause a slab to slide (again, unless the snow is very wet).

Why Do Slabs Fail?

Slabs usually fail or "release" when the load on the slab exceeds the bonding strength of a weak layer lying underneath. This is caused by a rapid buildup of stress upon the slab or by the internal weakening of the supporting layer. A slab avalanche can involve a single layer of wind-deposited snow that does not bond well to the layer beneath, or an entire winter's snowpack failing on a weak layer buried at the base of the snowpack. Slabs initially fail at the weakest point on a slope, but because the slab is under tension, the cohesive nature of the snow causes the slab to fracture along a defined line called a "crown line." In very hard slabs under a lot of tension, this may be accompanied by a loud "crack" like a rifle shot as the tension is released.

Direct-action Triggers

Most slab avalanches occur during or just after a storm when the new snow has accumulated faster than the snowpack can absorb the stresses. These are known as "direct-action" avalanches. As with other types of avalanches, victims of these slab avalanches generally trigger the slide that buries them. Additional loading from new snow or wind, as well as from a cornice release, are other examples of direct-action triggers. The snowpack will usually begin adjusting to a new load within forty-eight hours after a loading event, so avalanches release either during or immediately after a storm, making travel at those times unsafe.

Indirect-action Avalanche Triggers

Slabs also fail when a layer beneath the slab weakens. Avalanches that release due to internal weakening are called "indirect-action" avalanches. The primary cause of this type of avalanche is the development of weak crystals or bonds between layers within the snowpack. The weakening process is essentially the rotting of the snowpack from within. It is often characterized by the development of angular or faceted crystals, commonly known as "depth hoar." The hazard created by indirect-action triggers may actually increase with time after a storm, especially if the temperatures remain very cold or the snowpack is thin.

Warning! Sometimes a hard slab will be so strong that it can support itself even when part of the underlying weak layer collapses. When this happens, the slab will feel hollow underneath your feet or skis. This is a very dangerous condition! If the underlying layer collapses, there may be an audible *whoomph* as the air is pressed out. Due to the release of elastic tension in the layer, cracks may shoot out across the slope as the slab fails.

Wet and Dry Avalanches

Avalanches can also be characterized as being either "wet" or "dry" based on the amount of free water in the snow. Free water is liquid water, resulting from melting or rain, that is present between the frozen crystals of a snow layer. Wet avalanches occur when the temperature of the snow is above freezing and there is free water present in the snowpack. These slides generally move relatively slowly, although in the case of very wet snow, they can reach destructive speeds comparable to the force of a tidal wave. These wet slides often occur on warm spring days following fresh snowfall or rain, especially on more southerly slopes. Large wet slides commonly occur in the late spring with temperate climates similar to those in the Cascades or Sierra Nevada.

Dry avalanches can move much more quickly. Some low-density, powder-snow avalanches have been clocked at more than 200 miles per hour, with an airborne component that carries the destructive force of a hurricane. If the snow is fairly cohesive, these avalanches cover a large area. Large dry-snow avalanches commonly occur in continental climates such as those found in the Rocky Mountains.

Climax Avalanches

The term "climax avalanche" refers to slides that involve more than one layer of snow—sometimes taking the entire winter's snowpack down to the ground. Climax avalanches most often result from the collapse of a buried layer of depth hoar or the lubrication of a deeply buried sliding surface during periods of melt. These slides often occur as a result of a dramatic change in conditions, such as rain on the snowpack or prolonged periods of above-freezing temperatures.

Ice Avalanches

Of concern to glacier travelers are ice avalanches. These occur in icefalls or on other steep, glaciated slopes where a portion of the glacier calves off onto the slope below. These can be very destructive due to the massive amount of very dense material involved.

Extremely Large Avalanches

In mountain ranges with extreme relief, such as in Alaska, the Andes, and the Himalayas, there is added danger from extremely large avalanches. These have been observed falling thousands of vertical feet, crossing miles of flat glacier, and climbing up the other side of the valley to a remarkable height. The placement of your route, camps, caches, and rest stops should take this into consideration. Fortunately, most of us do not have to worry about these kinds of avalanches on our winter outings. If you plan to venture into these areas, take advanced avalanche courses prior to your trip and go with experienced companions.

Avalanche Preparedness

Before you begin traveling in avalanche country, you should consider the potential and current avalanche hazard. Most skiers and climbers are sensible enough to turn back in the face of extreme danger, but you'll need more information so the call can be made when conditions are not that obvious. The key to determining avalanche hazard is to gather as many clues as you can, and then relate this information to your goals and objectives. You may decide that your goals are not worth the risks and choose to abandon the trip, reevaluate and modify your goals, or find an alternate route. Of course, you might also decide that the rewards are worth the risk and go for it. The decision is up to you.

Trailhead Checklist
- Assess avalanche danger
- Choose a leader
- Determine group goals

- Agree on a rescue plan (see "Avalanche Rescue Techniques," p. 73)
- Practice a beacon search (see the search methods described in chapter 8)
- Tune your senses toward avalanche clues

PHYSICAL SIGNS OF AVALANCHE HAZARD

The most important sign of avalanche danger is the evidence of recent or past avalanches on similar slopes. Although this seems obvious, the clues are often overlooked. Evidence of natural avalanches on slopes slightly steeper and of similar aspect to the slope you are evaluating may mean that your chosen slope is prime avalanche hazard just waiting for a trigger. Snow dumping quickly from the branches of trees is a sign of very rapid settlement. The effect of gravity on the newly deposited snow causes the crystals to settle, or "densify." The crystals pack more closely together, compressing the layer of snowpack and increasing the density of the layer.

When the snow settles relatively slowly, the strength of the layer usually increases. However, when snow settles too quickly, the rapid densification of the overlying snow may cause a weaker layer buried deeper in the snowpack to fail. Other signs of avalanche hazard include cracks shooting out from under your skis, the feel of hollow snow, or rapid settling of the snow underfoot (often accompanied by an audible *whoomphing*). Any of these would indicate tension in the snowpack as well as a hidden weak layer.

Terrain Warning Signs

- Evidence of previous avalanches (branch-scoured trees, chutes, etc.)
- Steep slopes (more than thirty degrees)
- Changes in slope angle
- Open bowls, narrow gullies, and other terrain traps
- Leeward slopes subject to drifting snow

AVALANCHE EQUIPMENT

If you decide to travel in avalanche country, you should always be prepared whether or not you think there may be some danger. The moment you feel that awful drop of settling snow beneath your feet and the slope going *whoomph!* is no time to wish you had been more careful. Every member of the party should have a few essential pieces of equipment and know how to use them in an avalanche situation. As a minimum, everyone should have a functioning avalanche transceiver (beacon), shovel, and avalanche probe poles, as well as the skill to use them, confidence, and practice.

Basic Avalanche Equipment

- Avalanche transceiver (beacon)
- Sturdy lightweight shovel

- Collapsible avalanche probe pole
- Slope measurement device (Clinometer)
- Compass
- First-aid and winter survival/rescue gear
- Hand lens

Avalanche Transceivers

Avalanche transceivers or "beacons" are small radio transmitters/receivers that emit and receive a radio signal at a universal, unique frequency. With practice, transceivers can be used to quickly locate another unit (or more than one unit), even if it is buried deep in avalanche debris. Beacons have proven to be the best means for locating someone caught in an avalanche. Although they are relatively expensive, generally costing a few hundred dollars each, they should be considered economical insurance policies. Given the advances in technology that have been made in recent years, there is no good excuse for not using them when traveling in avalanche terrain. Of course, you need more than one unit for a successful rescue—each member of the group must use a beacon to ensure adequate coverage. Transceivers generally use "AA" or 9-volt transistor batteries. These batteries can last more than one hundred hours, but it is a good idea to replace the batteries regularly, as any reduction in signal strength could affect the success of a rescue.

At the beginning of a trip, before you even reach avalanche terrain, it is good protocol to switch your beacons to transmit, and leave them on for the remainder of the trip. Practicing a quick beacon search before you leave the trailhead, to make sure everyone is up to speed and their beacons work properly, is also a good idea. Similarly, it is good protocol to test the range of each of the units in both transmit and receive modes before heading out. Also at this point, choose a rescue leader for the group and review the basic plan for the day, including what would happen in the case of an avalanche accident.

The only frequency now available for avalanche transceivers is 457 kilohertz (kHz). This frequency replaced the old U.S. frequency of 2.275 kHz many years ago, and anyone still using these obsolete units should replace them immediately. The 457 kHz frequency provides much-improved signal transmission over greater distances, including through dense snow. Most of the units available today are completely digital or a combination of analog and digital signals. Many use microprocessors to register the direction and distance of the transmitting unit. As a result, the use of beacons is now much more intuitive, which in turn allows for more efficient and effective searches. Even so, it is still important to practice using these valuable tools so that if you ever have to use one, it will be second nature.

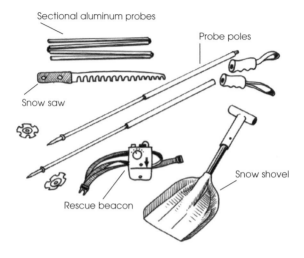

Figure 4. Proper avalanche gear

The goal in conducting a beacon search, whether it is in practice or the real thing, is to find the buried unit as quickly as possible. The time-honored search pattern for use with analog transceivers was called the "grid search." As the name implies, the search pattern followed a defined grid pattern, which followed progressively smaller, perpendicular passes to fine-tune the search. (See chapter 8, "Avalanche Rescue Techniques," for details on conducting a search.)

As noted above, the next generation of search patterns is much more intuitive and is based upon the improvements in dual antenna and processor technology, which allow much improved estimation of direction and distance or depth to a buried unit. Modern transceivers are still not quite as advanced as James Bond–style homing devices, i.e., high-tech gadgets that immediately point toward a buried transceiver, with the signal followed directly to a "dig here" message. However, we are getting close, and by the next edition of this book, that may become the standard. The new technology also makes it much easier to find multiple buried beacons, as they can differentiate between signals, allowing the searcher to find one beacon and then move on to the next.

Shovels

Your shovel has a variety of uses, but its main function is digging through avalanche debris when someone is caught in a slide. Therefore, the blade needs to be sturdy enough to cut through hard slab material or wet debris. The blade also needs to be large enough to move a large amount of snow quickly. However, if the shovel is too bulky, it will interfere with your normal travel and you might be tempted to leave it at home.

Instead, look for one of the special-use shovels available on the market. Most of them are made of heat-treated aluminum or Lexan plastic. The shaft needs to be very strong, preferably with a telescopic length adjustment—most offer a detachable blade. The handle should be comfortable to grip; a T- or D-shaped handle is best (see Figure 4, which shows a T-shaped handle). Shovels can also be used to dig pits for conducting snow-pit tests and to build snow shelters. Just remember that while some shovels work better for these tasks than others, the primary objective is to cut through dense debris and recover a buried friend. Be sure your shovel will work for that most important task.

Probes

An avalanche probe is another essential item. The probe can either be a separate piece of equipment, which looks like a long collapsible tent pole, or a pair of adjustable-length ski poles that together will form a long probe. A separate probe is an advantage because it will usually extend to a much greater length, and the narrow profile cuts through dense snow more easily. However, it is still an extra item to carry. Adjustable-length probe poles are very popular, and they help keep your gear to a minimum. The adjustable feature has nothing to do with their ability to probe, but can be a disadvantage if it causes the pole to slip while probing. Nonadjustable probes work better, although they are not as versatile. Modern carbon-fiber poles are lighter and easier to push into dense debris than traditional large-diameter aluminum poles.

Other Gear

Other than an avalanche transceiver, shovel, and probe, you really do not need much else in the way of specialized equipment. But there are a few simple tools that can help with the accuracy of your field observations. Number one is a clinometer, which measures slope angle. These are usually small plastic cards with a free-hanging arrow inside a capsule. By sighting the edge of the card against a slope, the arrow will hang down against the slope-angle scale (some compasses also have this feature). This can be critical in determining the difference between a relatively safe thirty-degree slope and a potentially fatal thirty-eight-degree slope—something that may be hard to gauge with the naked eye.

Other optional tools include a hand lens for checking snow crystals, a compass to determine the aspect of a slope, an altimeter to check the elevation of the slope, and a small dial-stem thermometer to check for temperature gradients within the snowpack. It is a good idea to carry a small notebook for note-taking and recording snowpack observations. You should also bring basic first-aid equipment to treat trauma and hypothermia in case of an accident, as well as extra clothes and survival gear to weather a potential overnight situation. See the FalconGuide *Wilderness Survival* by Suzanne Swedo for more information.

Avalanche Terrain

The best way to reduce avalanche hazard (the risk of being caught in an avalanche) is to avoid avalanche terrain. The most conservative approach is to treat all potential avalanche terrain as harboring hazardous conditions. Ask yourself, "Is the terrain capable of producing avalanches?" If the answer is yes, you need to ask yourself, "Do I really need to be here?" and if so, "What are the consequences if this slope slides?"

SLOPE

Avalanches only occur on slopes. If there is no slope, then it does not matter what the weather is doing or how unstable the snowpack is. The majority of avalanches occur on slopes from thirty to fifty degrees in steepness. The prime slope angle for slab avalanches is thirty-eight degrees. These would be black-diamond to double-black-diamond runs at a downhill ski area (see figure 5). Although this is quite steep, many backcountry skiers, climbers, and snowboarders consider this ideal terrain. Snowmobilers with powerful machines

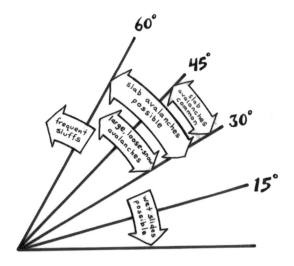

Figure 5. Slope angle

might also be tempted to "high mark" slopes this steep. Keep in mind that under certain circumstances, moderate-angled slopes can slide, and steeper slopes or cornices above can threaten even shallow-angled slopes.

TERRAIN

The type of terrain is important, too. Open bowls, tree-less slopes, and rocky couloirs (or gullies) are natural

Figure 6. Avalanche-flagged tree

avalanche paths. Narrow, confined drainages and creek beds are also potentially deadly terrain traps where even a small slide can deposit an impressive depth of debris. Ridgetops are generally safer, but you must be aware of potentially dangerous cornices. Rock outcrops and dense stands of trees on otherwise open slopes may provide "islands of safety," which offer localized areas of reduced hazard. Widely spaced trees, however, may be more hazardous than treeless slopes, as they provide minimal anchoring and great potential for traumatic injuries during a slide.

VEGETATIVE CLUES

Recognizing that a slope has slid in the past is a good clue that it could go again. Telltale vegetative clues like missing branches on the uphill side of trees (known as "flagging"; see figure 6), or trees bent over facing downhill, can also help identify a slope with a history of avalanches. Lobe-shaped cuts into dense timber, or defined trim-lines along the side of a gully, are other indications of the damaging size of past slides. The presence of invasive species like willows or aspens may also indicate frequent avalanche activity. The fact that a steep slope does not appear to have suffered a catastrophic avalanche does not mean it's safe, however: The area may have experienced a slide without damage to trees or other vegetation.

SLOPE CONFIGURATION

Changes in slope are another avalanche-hazard variable. Because gravity is constantly pulling on the snowpack, the greatest stress is found at the top of the slope or at areas where the slope angle changes. For this reason, convex rollovers, where the slope angle increases dramatically, are particularly dangerous. The slope just above a break-over point on a convex slope is under the greatest tension.

Compression stress is greatest at the bottom of convex slopes, and occasionally skiers have "tilted" a slab by overloading these areas. Slopes right below large rock outcrops or near buried bushes are likely failure points since very little tensile support exists above it. Buried bushes or small trees can also create weak points in the snowpack.

The underlying slope configuration is also important. Smooth slopes, like granite slabs, or steep grassy pitches provide minimal anchoring and can easily release the entire winter's snowpack if they become lubricated by meltwater percolating down and reaching these slick surfaces.

SLOPE ORIENTATION

The orientation of the slope to the wind and sun is critical. Leeward slopes (facing away from the prevailing wind) are rapidly loaded by heavy snowfall, even during periods of clear weather. You need to be aware of local winds that may flow in a different direction from the prevailing wind, too. Local winds frequently blow up- or down-canyon, carrying snow across the faces of canyon walls and ridges. As these crosswinds encounter local terrain, they may deposit the blowing snow on the leeward side of land features. If the winds are strong enough, a dangerous wind-formed slab may materialize in a very limited area.

The localized "cross-loading" of a slope can be very hard to detect. This is why you should be aware of shallow ridges, spurs, and rock outcrops, which are candidates for becoming localized slabs. In addition, warm winds can dramatically affect the stability of the snowpack by transferring heat to the surface layers.

The slope's orientation to the sun is also important. South-facing slopes receive the greatest amount of incoming solar radiation and tend to stabilize more quickly, but they may also release as a wet slide when the sun warms them. Sun balls, snowballs rolling down a slope that is being warmed by the sun, or small wet sluffs are signs of decreasing stability on sunny slopes. North-facing slopes are slower to feel the stabilizing effects of solar radiation and are more prone to the weakening effects of cold temperatures in midwinter. Shady north faces are likely places for faceted grains (depth hoar) to develop, rotting the pack over time. The opposite is true of slopes in the southern hemisphere.

TERRAIN TRAPS

Although wide, open powder bowls and steep couloirs offer the most obvious danger, and attraction, to back-country skiers, it is often a small, less-than-obvious slope on the approach (or at the end of the day) that catches the unwary winter traveler off guard. Terrain traps like confined gully bottoms are frequent sites of fatal avalanches—even a small slope can pile up a significant amount of debris. Slopes lying above exposed cliffs or crevasses can also be deadly.

Weather Considerations

If the terrain is capable of producing avalanches, the weather will provide the next set of clues to avalanche hazard. Before your trip, always check the weather forecasts for events that could affect snowpack stability. The primary weather considerations are precipitation, wind, and temperature. The main concern is how quickly a slope is being loaded, and how well the new layers of snow bond to each other. Heavy loading of new snow is an obvious concern, but not the only one. Drifting snow (wind loading) can greatly impact stability, even long after a storm. Moreover, any amount of rain on snow can increase the avalanche hazard; the same is true of warm winds, fog, and rapid changes in temperature.

Weather Warning Signs
- Heavy snowfall
- Strong winds and drifting snow

- Long periods of very hot or very cold temperatures
- Rain
- Warm winds
- Rapid changes in temperature

PRECIPITATION

The amount of new snow always affects the stability of the snowpack because of the additional weight (stress) added. The rate of loading (or deposition of new snow) is very important. If the snow accumulates faster than the snowpack can absorb this new stress, the slope may fail. New snow depositions of an inch or more per hour, or 12 inches or more in twenty-four hours, are definite signs that the avalanche hazard is increasing. New snow accumulations of 2 inches per hour, or 24 inches in twenty-four hours, are very serious indications of increasing avalanche hazard and may indicate high or even extreme danger.

DENSITY OF THE SNOW

Snow density is a critical factor in determining avalanche hazard, as it is more important to figure in the weight being applied to the snowpack than the inches of snow accumulation. Snow density is a measure of the water content or weight of the snow in relation to the volume of snow, and is usually referred to as a percentage. As a rule, new snow averages about

10 percent density (i.e., 10 percent water content, with air composing the other 90 percent). That equates to about six pounds per cubic foot. Areas with a more continental climate generally have very light snowfalls with average snow densities closer to 5 percent or less (3 lbs./ft. or more). Based on these figures we can see that a foot of heavy "Sierra Cement" would have over four times the density and relative impact on the snowpack as a foot of fluffy Colorado powder.

Avalanche statistics show that avalanche hazard increases significantly with the addition of more than 2 inches of water content in twenty-four hours. Compare this with the figures noted above. Of course, when this water comes in the form of wet snow or rain, it may not take even a twenty-four-hour loading at that rate to cause failure in the snowpack. (Free water in the snowpack can break down the bonds between crystals and percolate down in the snowpack and potentially lubricate a sliding surface like a buried ice layer.) When the snowpack receives 3 inches or more of water in a twenty-four-hour period, there is a high probability of widespread avalanche activity.

WIND

Even at low wind speeds, snow can be transported and localized. If there have been strong winds along with the recent snowfalls, downwind slopes near ridgetops will likely receive much more snow accumulation than

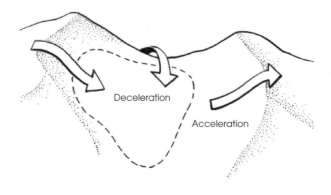

Figure 7. The effect of the wind

areas on flatter terrain. When wind speeds exceed about 10 miles per hour, snow can be transported. At wind speeds of more than 25 mph, the snow can be carried in the air by the wind. At wind speeds of more than 35 mph, strong eddying effects can develop on the leeward side of ridges.

Wind speeds increase on windward slopes and areas of packed snow. As wind accelerates, it erodes the windward snowpack, picking up loose snow and transporting it elsewhere. As the wind crosses a ridge or other terrain, the speed decreases and some of the transported snow is deposited on the leeward side (see figure 7). Sharp terrain features like cornices or narrow ridges often add to the eddying effect of strong winds. The densely deposited snow is often called a "snow pillow." Because the wind will continue to deposit the snow on the downwind side of a ridge, drifting continues as long as the wind blows, and snow can accumulate on leeward slopes even on a clear day.

TEMPERATURE

Rapid changes in temperature often trigger avalanches, even without additional new snow. Periods of very warm weather can weaken the snowpack by breaking down the bonds between the crystals, as well as promoting the movement of free water through the near-surface layers. Periods of very cold weather can make the snowpack brittle and cause recrystallization of near-surface or even deep snow layers. These weakening effects produce a poor foundation for future snow loading. Conversely, long periods of relatively moderate temperatures stabilize the snowpack by strengthening the bonds between layers.

The temperature of the snow itself is important. Slabs can form when a deposit of relatively warm cohesive snow or rimed crystals overlies a layer of cold, dry powder, and the new snow layer does not bond well with the old snow surface. The best bonds between snow layers form when storms begin warm and end cold. Storms that begin cold start with a weak formation and then become top-heavy with the addition of heavy, wet snow, forming weaker bonds. Cold layers of snow that are buried by warmer layers experience an extreme local "temperature gradient" and often undergo rapid change, quickly becoming faceted crystals. This process essentially "rots" the snowpack over a short period of time. Read more about this topic in chapter 5.

Getting to Know
the Snowpack

For a complete assessment of avalanche hazard, you need to know the snowpack. Familiarity with the snowpack means being aware of surface conditions, as well as what is going on below the surface, perhaps all the way to the ground. Methods of determining how changes in the snowpack affect stability are addressed in chapter 6, "Testing the Snow." This chapter discusses the physical processes that lead to changes in the composition of the snowpack, as well as the stresses that act upon the snowpack, thus affecting stability.

SNOWPACK

As soon as a snowflake falls from the sky, it undergoes changes. Air temperature, humidity, wind speed, riming (free water freezing to the crystal), and other weather factors combine to produce the snow crystal that eventually lands on the ground. Once on the ground, a variety of changes occur, depending on how quickly it becomes buried, as well as the temperature, humidity, depth, and location of the snowpack. With a little experience and a hand lens, you can learn to identify these crystals, as well as the physical processes that brought them to their present state.

Taking identification one step further, you can eventually learn how to read the layers within the snowpack and gain an understanding of how all of this affects the stability of the snowpack. The entire snowpack undergoes changes over the course of a winter, too. Each successive loading event produces layers with distinct properties. These layers can be several feet thick or so thin that they are difficult to detect. Depending on the continued weather patterns, these layers may become stronger or weaker, as can the bonds that develop between these layers.

STABILIZING PROCESSES

Following a storm, the new snow usually begins to undergo significant changes within the first few days, and the snowpack tends to stabilize. The pull of gravity on the individual crystals leads to an increase in the bonding between the crystals and an overall gain in the strength of the layer. Given moderately warm temperatures and stable weather conditions, the hazard of this layer becoming an avalanche decreases rapidly over time. In warmer climates, this may take only twenty-four to forty-eight hours, but in colder climates this process is much slower, and the snowpack may take weeks to stabilize. Under optimal conditions, with moderate temperatures and relatively deep snow coverage, there is little temperature difference over the depth of the snowpack (i.e., less than one degree Celsius per 10 centimeters of depth).

The physics of these conditions cause water vapor to be transferred from convex surfaces to concave surfaces, with a net *decrease* in crystal size and a net *increase* in the strength of the layer. There is a general rounding of the crystals, and strong bonds between adjacent crystals are formed, which are referred to as "ice necks." These crystals are frequently referred to as "rounds" and are an indicator of developing stability in that layer. The natural settlement of the snowpack augments this process due to the weight of the snowpack and the pull of gravity. As the crystals settle and become more tightly packed, the pressure on the snowpack creates bonds between crystals due to the "sintering" (or pressure bonding) process. This densification generally works to promote stability of the snowpack, unless settlement occurs too quickly.

When rapid settlement occurs, the densification of the surface layer puts great stress on the tensile strength of the layer, possibly causing failure, resulting in an avalanche. For example, when the sun first hits a freshly loaded slope on a warm spring morning, the rapid input of heat can actually decrease the strength of the layer by breaking down the bonds between crystals and increasing the tensile strain on the layer. If this stress exceeds the snowpack's ability to absorb the stress, an avalanche will occur.

As the bonds between the crystals break down and meltwater begins to move freely in the layer, individual crystals may slide down the slope, picking up others as they go, like a cartoon snowball. These "rollers" or "sun balls" are an indication of the snowpack's decreasing stability and increasing avalanche hazard. The larger the sun balls become, the greater the likelihood of a wet-snow avalanche.

The same effect occurs with rain, fog, or warm wind. Changes in the temperature and humidity of the layer cause rapid settlement and movement of free water in the surface layers. After the sun leaves the slope, the layer will gain strength again by refreezing.

THE MELT-FREEZE (MF) PROCESS

When temperatures are well above freezing, the bonds between snow crystals begin to melt, producing free water that starts to percolate down through the snowpack until it refreezes. When the water refreezes, it creates very strong bonds between crystals, as well as increasing the size of the receiving crystal. Therefore, the layer's strength decreases as the bonds melt, and then increases again as the bonds freeze. As long as nighttime temperatures are cold enough to allow refreezing, this process will eventually lead to a very stable snowpack.

In most areas the MF process is limited to spring, but in areas of lower elevation (or lower latitude), this can occur throughout the winter. This is why mountaineers have long known that it is safer to travel early in the day when the snowpack is frozen solid, rather than late in the afternoon when the possibility of a wet avalanche is greatly increased.

However, during periods when temperatures do not drop below freezing, the melting process can continue even at night, allowing water to percolate down through the snowpack until it reaches a weak layer or a potential sliding surface, such as a buried ice lens or crust layer. The water may lubricate this layer, increasing the chances of a wet slide. When these "melt-melt" conditions persist for more than a day or two, as often happens in spring, then large-scale avalanches can occur at any time, possibly releasing the entire winter's snowpack to the ground. At these times, it is almost impossible to predict avalanche hazard, and it is best to wait in a safe location or abandon your tour.

DESTABILIZING PROCESSES

Shallow snowpack coupled with cold temperatures present the opportunity for a temperature gradient, or differential, to develop. This occurs between individual layers, i.e., when a warm snowfall is followed by a very cold storm, or over the entire snowpack, when the ground remains close to freezing while the air temperature is much colder. A significant temperature gradient can quickly decrease the strength of a layer or the entire snowpack by breaking down the bonds between individual crystals and between layers themselves. If this differential is greater than one degree Celsius per 10 centimeters of depth, then a significant temperature gradient exists. This condition is common for all areas early in the season. In continental climates, like in the Rocky Mountains, this situation can persist throughout much of the winter.

The physics of vapor transfer are almost the opposite under the faceting process compared to the more benign rounding process. Vapor is transferred from concave to convex surfaces, resulting in the development of larger, more angular crystals with clearly visible facets. These new crystals are frequently referred to as "faceted crystals" or simply "squares." The crystal growth often comes at the expense of the bonds between the crystals, leading to a general weakening of the layer. With the faceting process, the bottom line is that there is an *increase* in crystal size and a net *decrease* in the strength of that layer.

Snowpack Processes

- Stabilizing conditions: decrease in crystal size with net increase in layer strength
- MF conditions: increase in crystal size with daily change in layer strength
- Destabilizing conditions: increase in crystal size with net decrease in layer strength

Depth Hoar

When faceted crystals develop deep in the snowpack, they were historically referred to as "depth hoar" crystals. When the change occurs in near-surface layers, the new crystals are called "freeze-dried powder." Because these angular, faceted crystals have relatively no internal cohesion or bonding, they behave much like sugar crystals and are frequently referred to as "sugar snow." Mature faceted crystals can be quite large (up to 5 millimeters or larger) and may be cup- or pyramidal-shaped. These weak crystals can become a very serious concern when they are buried under subsequent snowfalls.

Like a house of cards, a layer of faceted crystals can support a fair amount of weight in compression, but may be very weak in shear. Once developed, these layers remain buried within the snowpack, creating a weak foundation for future loading. Once disturbed, these weak layers will collapse just like a house of cards, leaving no support for the overlying layers. As the air is pressed out of the layer, there is often an audible "whoomph" and sudden drop of the surface layers. Faceted crystal layers are often the trigger for a slab avalanche, and many avalanche victims added the additional stress that caused a weak layer of faceted crystals to fail.

Surface Hoar

Another type of faceted crystal is known as "surface hoar." Unlike the three-dimensional structure of sugar snow that develops due to changes in existing snow crystals, surface hoar is two-dimensional (like a snowflake). Surface hoar crystals are equivalent to winter dew and similar to the hoar-frost crystals that grow in your freezer or on your car window. Water vapor in the air contacts the relatively colder, drier snow surface and freezes into the same crystalline structure as snow.

After a cold, clear night these crystals can be seen sparkling on the surface of the snowpack. Undisturbed, these crystals grow quite large and persist for long periods, even when buried by subsequent snowfall. These layers are often very thin and difficult to detect, but they are a concern if they form a weak layer that becomes a sliding surface in the future.

STRESSES AND STRENGTHS

The layers within the snowpack are affected by a variety of factors that make the snowpack either stronger or weaker. The three main factors that affect the snowpack are compression, tension, and friction. The stability of the snowpack will depend on the magnitude of each of these factors, as applied by gravity or external forces, and the ability of the snowpack to resist them. As noted previously, the pull of gravity can either strengthen the snowpack by packing the crystals closer together, or rip it apart by rapid settling or general fatigue. When we add a slope component, things can become complex, especially if there are variations in the slope, but it may serve to look at these factors individually.

Compression

Compression stress is generally greatest at the bottom of a slope or in areas where the angle decreases, and where the snowpack is trying to support the weight of the slope above. Compression stress also occurs at the point where a climber or skier compresses snow crystals with a step or ski track, testing the ability of the layer to resist compression. Obviously denser layers will have greater inherent strength than less dense layers. If the compression strength of the snowpack is compromised by cutting, such as by a ski or snowmobile track, the entire slope above can release because the support has been removed. This is sometimes called "tilting the slab."

Tension

Tension in the snowpack is obvious and can be expressed as the elastic strength of the snowpack or individual layer. The elastic strength of a layer depends on the air and snow temperature, the water content of the snow, and the amount and intensity of stress applied to the layer. Given relatively warm temperatures and wet snow, a layer can accommodate an incredible amount of elastic deformation, especially if the stress is applied slowly (as is the case with gravity). However, given cold temperatures and dry snow, the layer will be much more brittle; a small amount of stress may cause the slope to fail dramatically, often with a loud "crack," like a rifle shot.

Tension and the force of gravity are greatest at the top of the snowpack or in places where the slope angle increases; therefore support from below is reduced. The greatest hazard from slab failure occurs at these points. The ability of the snowpack to remain in place on steep slopes depends on the elastic, bonding strength of individual crystals resisting the pull of gravity. Although some strength comes from the side and bottom of the slope, the most stress is applied at the steepest point, which is often near the top.

The elastic nature of a snow layer can be seen when snow gradually slides off a roof. Without disturbance, the snow may even curl up under the eaves, but if it is disturbed, it will fail dramatically. The same is true in the backcountry; if a slope is under extreme tension and then fails, it will snap like a rubber band and a crack will shoot across an entire slope in a matter of seconds, followed closely by a large slab avalanche.

Friction

Shear stress is applied by the release of either tension or compression and is directly affected by the friction or bonding between two layers. Layers of different density will react differently to shear forces. The greatest hazard occurs when a dense layer overlies a weaker layer. In this case, the dense layer is more inclined to move cohesively (relative to the weaker layer below) and the bond between the two layers fails. Other common sources of poor shear strength include slick surfaces like buried crusts or ice layers, a thin layer of "graupel" or "ball-bearing" snow crystals, surface hoar, or a layer of faceted crystals.

Ultimately, the shear strength of the bond between layers determines whether a slope will fail. Many times a slope will fail in tension, with a crack shooting across the slope, but the friction (or shear strength) between the layers keeps the slab from releasing. This is a very scary situation, but much better than having the slab fail and take the whole hillside down with you on it. Testing the shear strength between two layers is the best way to determine slope stability. This is covered in the next chapter.

Testing the Snow

SIMPLE TESTS OF SNOWPACK STABILITY

To learn more about what is going on under the surface of the snow, try a variety of quick stability tests that can be done without taking your skis off. The simplest is a snow pit test that uses just your ski pole. By pressing the basket into the snow you can get a feel for the thickness of layers and their relative densities (see figure 8). In good light you can look down the hole and see what is happening below the surface, or bring up some crystals from each layer on your pole basket. This test is very quick and allows you to easily track changes in the snowpack as you move from place to place.

Signs of Unstable Snowpack
- Recent avalanche activity on slopes with similar aspect and angle
- Cracks or settling ("whoomphing" sound) underfoot

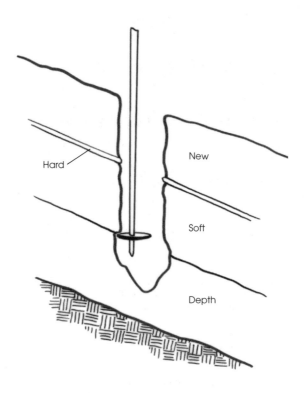

Hard

New

Soft

Depth

Figure 8. Layering of snow

- Strong layers overlying weak layers
- Snow tests indicating weak shear strength
- Faceted crystals buried deep in the snowpack

If you are curious about a layer, scoop out a tiny pit with your glove. Many "minipits" are often better than just one more formal pit on an isolated slope. The important thing is to gather as much information as possible and relate it to your other observations. However, if you are going to spend some time on a slope, the best way to get a handle on the local stability of the snowpack is to dig a pit.

Other on-ski checks include simple tests like cutting small wedges of snow with a kick turn, checking for release of the wedge of snow between the tracks. This is a good indication of slab conditions and possibly poor bonding between near-surface layers. Stepping uphill of a traverse ski track and pushing down onto the cut track will also provide a graphic test of near-surface conditions.

Testing small, safe slopes on skis is one of the best ways to give you a more realistic idea about the stability on nearby slopes of similar aspect. Observing how deeply you sink into the snow on skis or on foot gives you idea about the density of the snow and how much snow might potentially be involved in a slide. However, test skiing must be used with a great deal of caution. The same can be said for breaking off cornices to evaluate snowpack layers. Done safely, test skiing gives you an indication of relative stability.

MORE-INVOLVED TESTS

All of the simple snowpack stability tests provide rapid, ongoing updates and assessments to add to your other stability clues and observations. However, if you are still unsure about a given slope, or concerned about buried weak layers, you should dig a pit. A snow pit is an excellent way to learn more about the snow-pack history of that particular slope by identifying individual layers and checking the strength of the bonds between the layers. You may want to measure the depth of the snowpack, since snow may have buried any potential anchors such as shrubs or boulders. Essentially, you are testing for both depth and the exis-tence of anchors, but if the snow is more than 4 feet deep, most anchors are buried. Look for weak layers or situations where denser layers lie over less dense layers. In addition, look for potential sliding sur-faces such as buried ice crusts or pockets of faceted crystals.

For a better indication of the shear strength between layers, use a shovel shear test. However, if you have the time, the best way of determining how your pres-ence will affect the stability of the snowpack is to per-form a Rutschblock Stability Test. This test, also known as the Swiss Army Ski Test, produces quantifiable results, which can provide the final word on whether a slope is a go or no-go. These tests are described below.

DIGGING A SNOW PIT

Depending on your goals, snow pits do not have to be very elaborate. Digging a quick "hasty" pit might take only fifteen or twenty minutes, whereas a more formal pit may take up to an hour. In either case, your pit should be deep enough so you can investigate the layers you are most concerned about. About 3 to 4 feet should be deep enough unless fractures in the snow are running deeper than that, or you know there is a buried weak layer that could cause trouble. You will want to make the pit at least that wide, too, to allow for a couple of shovel shear tests to gauge the strength of the bonds between layers.

Make sure to dig your pit in a safe area that still reflects the conditions of the slope you are worried about as closely as possible. You don't want to dig the pit in the starting zone of an avalanche path, but you also don't want to dig a pit on a low angled slope in the trees well below your chosen bowl, either. The information you gather from the pit will be most useful if the pit is dug on a slope that exceeds thirty degrees in steepness. The closer you get to the suspect slope in angle, terrain, and location, the more accurate the information will be. Also make sure that the pit is not over any bushes or rocks, which might provide false information. The better the location, the better the results.

Before you begin digging, mark out the area you are planning to excavate. If you are planning to do a Rutschblock Test (see p. 59), make the pit at least a ski-length wide. Smooth the walls as much as possible so you can easily distinguish individual layers. For the best information, make the pit walls and the face of the pit perpendicular. Digging into the slope from below will be easier and more efficient than digging a hole straight down. You will also want to make sure that your pack or loose items are off to the side to avoid burying them.

The Snow Pit Test

1. Dig pit with shovel.
2. Smooth sides of pit with shovel or ski.
3. Run a plastic card down wall to feel layers.
4. Check relative hardness of layers by hand and finger probes (see chart on p. 56).
5. Watch for denser layers overlying less dense or weaker layers.

CHECKING THE SNOW

As you dig, look for red-flag situations such as denser layers overlying weaker layers, hard ice lenses, or weak, faceted crystals on top of a smooth crust. How the snow behaves as you dig the pit will supply a few important clues. As mentioned before, it is not usually necessary to dig the pit more than 3 to 4 feet deep. (However, in continental climates you may want to dig a little deeper.) If it is early or late in the season and you suspect deep slab or layers of depth hoar, you may want to dig to the ground.

Once you have dug the pit, check for individual layers by running a plastic card or even your finger down the face of the wall. Mark significant layers, particularly buried crusts or layers of faceted crystals, for later identification. Another method for identifying layers is using a whisk broom or your glove to brush the surface of the pit wall. Using consistent strokes, you can highlight layers as you go down the wall of the pit. Of particular interest are denser layers that overlie weaker layers, or weak crystals that spill out like sugar. A small hand lens or magnifying glass will help you recognize individual crystal types.

GAUGING THE RELATIVE DENSITY

Once you're satisfied that you've identified the important layers, check the relative hardness or density of the layers using your fist, four fingers together, one finger only, a pencil, and, finally, a knife. This test uses relative resistance to penetration as an indication of density. First, try pushing your fist into a layer. If it does not go in all the way, try using four fingers. If you

SNOW HARDNESS TEST

Object necessary to penetrate snow	Hardness of snow
Fist	Very soft
Four fingers	Soft
One finger	Medium
Pencil	Hard
Knife	Very hard
Ice	Impenetrable

still cannot get them in all the way, try one finger. A layer that requires one finger to puncture it is a relatively hard layer. If the layer is too hard for your finger, try a pencil, then eventually a knife. Anything too hard for a knife to penetrate is classified an ice layer. If you have the right tools, you can calculate the actual weight or density of a layer. The chart above provides a rough measure of relative density or hardness of the top layer of snow by determining what method will penetrate the layer.

Ideally, the layers within the pack should become progressively harder or denser with depth, like a pyramid with a strong base that supports the layers above. Snowpack that gets progressively softer with depth is very unstable—like an upside-down pyramid, precariously balanced on its point. For example, a thick layer with pencil density sitting on top of a layer with fist density is a definite cause for concern, especially if the fist-density layer was buried a couple of feet deep. This condition is called a density inversion. Density inversions are known to create deep slab instability.

SHOVEL SHEAR TEST

To identify the shear strength of the bonds between layers, use the shovel shear test. To perform this test, isolate a column of snow with your shovel, a snow saw, or a ski tail, about a shovel-blade wide and shovel-blade deep, on the rear wall of the snow pit (see figure 9). Isolating the column completely ensures that you are testing only the shear strength and not additional strength factors. Place the blade of the shovel in the cut at the back of the column and slide it down the back of the column, trying not to lever out on the column. When the blade is all the way down, pull straight out on the column. If poor shear strength exists between two layers, the column will fail and release cleanly at its base.

The problem with the shovel shear test is that it can exaggerate weakness in the pack, provide rather subjective results, and may not identify the layer that you should be most concerned about. For example, curved-bladed shovels have a tendency to lever on the column. Subtle outward pressure on the handle

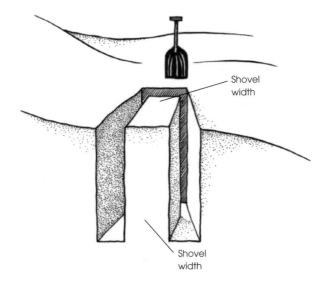

Shovel
width

Shovel
width

Figure 9. Shovel test

can also make the hazard seem greater than it is. You
may have several shear failures in a column or only
failure at the base. However, by using consistent methods on a number of columns and then applying that
information to other observations, you can still gain
valuable information from this test.

The Shovel Shear Snow Test

1. Follow the steps on p. 54 for digging a snow pit.
2. Isolate a column of snow with a shovel, saw, or your ski tail.
3. Cut the back of the column with your ski tail or saw.
4. Look for layer failure as you gently pull out the column with your shovel blade or ski tail.

STUFFBLOCK SHEAR TEST

A similar test requires a stuff sack and a fishing scale. Weigh out a set amount of snow, usually five or ten pounds, in the stuff sack. Drop the sack from progressively higher positions onto an isolated column of snow, like the one in the shovel test, until a layer fails to give you reasonably objective results. Alternately, you can continue to add more weight and drop the sack from the same height each time until a layer fails. This test is a small-scale version of the widely accepted Rutschblock Test.

RUTSCHBLOCK TEST

The Rutschblock Test is the most accurate and relevant test for safely determining snowpack stability. The goal of this test is to see how the shear strengths of the layers within the block react to a given amount of stress (i.e., your weight on skis). Since your weight

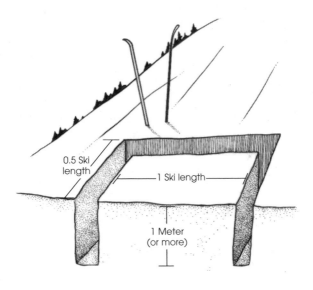

Figure 10. The Rutschblock Test

on skis is constant, this test can be performed several times and gives you a good sense of how your presence will affect the stability of the snowpack. However, this test still only provides a rough estimate of stability. To be on the safe side, treat all test data as inconclusive and always back it up with other observations.

The Rutschblock Stability Test

Step 1: Dig a large test snow pit at least a ski-length wide. (See figure 10).

Step 2: Make sure the face of the pit is smooth.

Step 3: Cut up into the hill about half a ski length on both sides and down the back, isolating a large block of snow. (Cut deep enough to involve all relevant layers. If you cut the front a little wider than the back, the block slides out more easily without binding on the sides, giving you a clearer picture of failure.)

Step 4: After isolating the block, the following steps provide an objective scale of stability.

4.1 Put your skis on and approach the top of the block from the side. If the block slides at this point, conditions are extremely unstable and the slope should not be skied.

4.2 Once you are directly above the block, step gently onto the top of the block. If the block releases at this point, conditions should be considered very unstable, and again you should stay off the slope.

4.3 Once you are safely onto the block, drop your weight onto both feet without jumping. If the block releases at this point, conditions should be considered unstable; it would be wise to stay off the slope.

4.4 Now, take one cautious jump and land on both feet. If the block releases at this point, conditions should be considered fairly unstable. Prudence would dictate that you stay off the slope. However, you may choose to ski the slope if other clues do not indicate instability, and you practice all of your safe-travel tricks. (See "Safe Travel Basics" on p. 66.)

4.5 Try two solid jumps, landing on both feet. If the block fails at this point, it is difficult to tell if the slope is stable or not. Use your best judgment along with other observations to back up your decision.

4.6 If the block releases only after multiple jumps or . . .

4.7 . . . not at all, the slope is reasonably stable. However, normal precautions should still be used.

It is important to note that while the Rutschblock Test provides very useful information, it does not provide a complete picture. Many people will use this test merely to confirm the sum of their observations, as well as to make sure they are not missing something important. No matter how many tests you perform, you will still have to base your decision to venture into avalanche terrain on your overall judgment of stability. Unfortunately, the results of a Rutschblock Test in borderline conditions are often not conclusive, either.

When instability is obvious, the Rutschblock performs well. However, when things are moderately stable, the tests generally show this, too. You still have to make the call. When in doubt about snow stability, treat the terrain with respect and stick to lower angled slopes. Remember, you have to live (or die) with your decision.

The Human Factor

The final factor, and really the most important one in determining and controlling avalanche hazard, is the human factor. Unlike the other three factors, this involves a series of subjective decisions determined more by our ego, psychology, and feelings than by pure science or quantifiable physical factors. It depends on how we feel and how we interact with others as much as our experience and education.

Much of the current research in avalanche hazard has gone into analyzing the decision-making process, including identifying and assessing the factors that lead people to make poor decisions regarding travel in avalanche terrain. Often referred to as "heuristic traps," there is a distinct difference between hierarchical decision making (i.e., recognizing the combination of terrain, weather, and snowpack conditions) and "heuristics," which refer to using "rule-of-thumb" shortcuts (i.e., relying on what normally works) to address complex situations. This often results in missing important clues and increasing our risk by assuming conditions are safer than they really are based on past experience. The flip side of this process involves taking the time to assess the situation and making specific analytical decisions to assess and increase our safety.

Limit your exposure. If you must travel in avalanche terrain during periods of questionable stability, make sure that only one person is exposed to danger at a time; therefore, someone will be available to affect a rescue if something goes wrong. Make sure that the group communicates its goals, desires, and fears, and everyone has the proper equipment, including beacons, shovels, and probe poles.

Safe travel in avalanche country involves a combination of common sense, route-finding skills, accurate assessment of avalanche danger, and conservative travel practices. Recognize avalanche terrain and avoid this terrain when snow conditions are unstable.

Most people trigger the avalanche that catches them; their presence tipped the balance of stability. Usually the victim ignored not just one but a number of clues that should have told him to stay clear of avalanche terrain. In spite of these clues, some foolishly place themselves in harm's way. Your safety and that of the others in your group depends on your ability to recognize when to play it safe. In some cases it may take more than just the weight of one additional skier to start the slide. It may take two, three, or ten. The same goes for snowmobilers. A slope may handle one snowmobile and a rider but may not support two without failing.

If you have a chance, test-ski a short adjacent slope with similar aspect and steepness, but less exposure. Be especially wary of cracks forming in the snow, "whoomphing" noises, and settlement under your skis. If you have any doubts about the stability of the snowpack, take the time to dig a pit and perform a Rutschblock or other stability test to learn more about the snowpack.

SAFE TRAVEL BASICS

- Avoid steep terrain (slopes over thirty degrees) if there is any potential hazard.
- Avoid potential trigger zones. Most people trigger the avalanche that buries them. (See "Avalanche Triggers," p. 5)
- Give the slope a chance to settle. Most avalanches occur within forty-eight hours of a storm or period of drifting snow.
- Take advantage of safer terrain, like dense timber, wide valley bottoms, and broad ridgetops.
- Avoid confined gullies, open bowls, leeward slopes, and areas of steep slope changes.

- Treat all potential avalanche terrain as though it is ready to fail.
- Choose a leader, make a rescue plan, and develop alternate routes and contingency plans.
- Switch beacons to transmit at the beginning of the day.
- Tighten zippers, gloves, and clothes.
- Remove ski-pole straps.
- Travel one at a time, with all eyes on the person crossing the slope.
- Don't assume a slope is safe if one person crossed it without sliding.
- Move quickly to and from safer zones or "islands of safety."
- Enter a potentially dangerous slope as high as you can.
- Think of the consequences of being caught in an avalanche. What would you do?

WHEN TO GO

Avalanches generally release during or just after a storm, as the slope is trying to regain stability by balancing the stresses. Therefore, the timing of your trip (or your travel during a trip) has a lot to do with your safety. If you can wait up to forty-eight hours after the storm or loading event has ended, you will greatly improve your odds by giving the slope a chance to stabilize and adjust to the new load.

Impatient powder-hounds often become avalanche victims; ask yourself if first tracks are worth dying for. Even in the worst avalanche areas, most slopes are relatively safe perhaps 90 percent of the time. If you make sure that you do not go into the wrong place during the other 10 percent of the time, you will be able to travel safely almost 100 percent of the time.

ROUTE FINDING

Learn to recognize "avalanche country" and choose a route that avoids it. Stay clear of obvious avalanche terrain by taking advantage of dense timber, rock outcrops, broad ridges, wide valley bottoms, and various exposures to the sun and wind. (Take advantage of sun or temperature factors and travel at night or only early in the morning. If temperatures are too warm, avoid cornices if at all possible.)

Have an alternate route agreed upon in advance in case of unforeseen contingencies. Sometimes it's better to sacrifice time and drop down to the valley floor or climb to the ridgeline rather than cross the middle of a slope. Above all else, you want to avoid a route that takes you into the starting (trigger) zone or lingers in a likely deposition area.

MAKE A PLAN

Plan your route ahead of time based on topographic maps, local information, and the group's experience. Choose a leader and make sure that everyone has agreed to the plan. Figure out the safe places to stop and have an escape route in case an avalanche starts. Be prepared to turn back or take another route if the danger seems too great.

BE PREPARED

Before making the commitment to enter avalanche terrain, take the time to get your personal gear in order. Tighten up all zippers, gloves, and loose clothing and make sure that you are well padded and insulated if caught. If you're wearing a light pack, cinch it down, too; it can help pad your torso in the event of a tumbling slide through rocks or timber. If you have a heavy, full-size pack, you might want to release the waistbelt and sternum strap.

It is a good idea to remove the straps of your ski poles, as well as runaway leashes on your skis or board so you can get rid of them. If it is possible, loosen your bindings so they will come off in a slide. Nonrelease bindings on telemark skis or a snowboard can be deadly. It is much more difficult to remain on the surface of the slide with skis on. Not only will boards attached to your feet increase the chance for leg trauma, they will also act as anchors, dragging you down.

SAFE DOWNHILL TRAVEL

Although it might seem like the macho thing to do, don't jump off a cornice, drop into the middle of a bowl, or climb up the throat of a narrow gully unless you are absolutely sure of the slope's stability. Imagine the slope as a minefield, and choose a route that avoids trigger points. Be aware of subtle changes in slope or aspect, and try to move quickly to and from each "island of safety." Wooded slopes are generally safer than open slopes, but that does not mean they're hazard free. If you can ski through the trees, an avalanche can maneuver through them, too. Try to stick to the tops of ridges rather than the middle of open bowls or exposed gullies.

Use subtle terrain features to give yourself every advantage. Find the lowest angled line, the most sheltered slope, the densest timber. Avoid potential avalanche-trigger zones and terrain traps like narrow gullies, open bowls and cirques, obvious leeward slopes, and known slide paths. Places where the slope angle changes are often trigger points, especially convex slope rollover points. When skiing down a bowl, the first skier should choose a line that hugs the side of the bowl. Each additional skier should pick a line next to the previous track, gradually moving farther out into the bowl.

While you are skiing, never let your guard down. Even after you have made it halfway down a slope, you may hit a trigger point and start a slide.

If you must cross a threatening slope, do so as high up as you can. This pertains to skiing into a bowl, too; if a slide starts, most of it will be below your skis, and there is less chance of being buried. Whenever possible, take the time to travel one at a time. This limits risk to one person at a time, leaving the rest of the group available as rescuers and putting less stress (or weight) on the slope. All eyes of the party should follow the skier to note his or her position in case of an avalanche.

SAFE CLIMBING

When climbing up a slope, everyone should follow the same track. Sometimes a line straight up the slope is the safest route, since it puts the least amount of stress on the snowpack. When traversing across a slope, the first person should pick a line that traverses between "islands of safety." Remember, just because one or more skiers have made it safely up, across, or down a slope, it does not mean the slope is completely safe. In the case of a hard slab, it may take the weight and cutting action of a number of climbers or skiers to weaken the slab before it collapses. Always be thinking of the avalanche hazard.

SAFE SNOWMOBILING

All of the previous recommendations also hold true for other winter recreationists. However, there is one special note on snowmobile safety: The challenge of "high marking" or riding high up a steep slope on a snowmobile is inherently hazardous and leaves few options for safe-travel considerations.

Avalanche Rescue Techniques

Nature provides us with many clues to snowpack stability that don't require you to pull out your shovel and dig a pit in the snow. The most important and most obvious sign of instability is recent avalanches on similar slopes to the one you plan to explore. Natural avalanches on steeper slopes will tell you that your chosen slope, if it is also as steep, is primed and waiting for you—the trigger. However, the lack of natural avalanches does not mean that the coast is clear. Other physical signs of instability include rapid settlement of the snow out of trees or off of rocks, cracks shooting out from under your boots or skis, snow that feels hollow underfoot, and "whoomphing" sounds as you travel. To really be sure about what is going on under the surface, you'll need to dig in and test the snowpack.

FATAL ATTRACTION

Avalanches kill in two ways. First, a person can receive traumatic injuries during the slide. A slide path that takes the skier over cliffs, rock outcrops, or crevasses presents the greatest threat. The wrenching action of the snow in motion can also cause injuries, especially with hard slabs or dense, wet snow. Unfortunately, sometimes even the quickest rescue efforts will not help someone who is seriously injured in a slide. About one-third of all avalanche fatalities are due to trauma, usually to the head and neck.

Second, but of equal concern, is the possibility that a buried victim may suffocate. A person caught in a slide will often inhale or swallow a mouthful of snow, which blocks the airway. Once the slide comes to a stop, you'll find that debris surrounds the person. In wet snow, the debris can refreeze like cement, leaving little room for movement. In either case, a limited amount of air is available for the victim to breathe; the pressure of the snow makes it hard for the person to expand her chest to breathe.

This is why time is so critical in rescue efforts. Once the snow sets up, which happens almost immediately, it becomes practically impossible for a person to dig himself out or even move his arms up to his face to clear an airspace. A person without adequate air can survive for only about five minutes. A review of avalanche accidents shows that the chances of survival diminish greatly if the victim is completely buried; the odds of survival are cut in half after thirty minutes have elapsed. In addition, the deeper a person is buried, the smaller his chance of being rescued alive. That is why rescue efforts need to begin as quickly and efficiently as possible.

IF YOU ARE CAUGHT

When the snow is just starting to release, you may have a chance to escape. Stay on your feet if possible. If the snow is sliding out from under your skis, scramble uphill or grab a tree. If you are in the middle of a slide, try to ski out to the side—that way, you can avoid the main mass of the slide. Do not try to ski or ride out ahead of the slide—avalanches move very fast and will likely catch you.

As you are caught, shout to your companions, alerting them to your predicament. Giving them a clue to your position is very important if you are buried. If you are caught, try to keep your mouth closed and breathe through your nose if possible. Put all of your energy into fighting the slide. Get rid of your skis and poles if you can. If you are knocked off your feet, try to swim to the surface. Positioning yourself in the upper part of the slide may keep you from being completely buried.

The avalanche will eventually begin to slow. As a victim, you have a brief second or two to reach the surface before the snow sets up. Unless you are deeply buried or unconscious, you will probably know which way is up. Make your swimming motions in the upward direction. Try desperately to push your head, hand, or arm above the surface. Any clue to your position will greatly improve your odds.

As the snow halts, make an airspace in front of your mouth. Do anything to keep the snow from packing tightly around you. Keep calm and remember, if you have practiced conservative skiing, your partners have already begun your rescue. If you hear your friends searching above, go ahead and shout; they may be able to hear you. Otherwise, remain as quiet as you can.

WHAT TO DO IF YOU'RE CAUGHT IN AN AVALANCHE

- Shout to your companions.
- Stay on your feet.
- Ski to the side, not out in front of the avalanche.
- If you are swept down, try to swim to the surface.
- As the slide comes to a halt, put one hand in front of your face to make an air pocket and thrust the other hand toward the surface.

IF ONE OF YOUR PARTNERS IS CAUGHT

If one of your partners is caught, you need to act quickly and positively. Your actions over the next several minutes may mean the difference between life and death for your friend.

Warning! Before you do anything, you need to make sure the area is not threatened by other slide paths, and, if so, you may decide to post a watchman and coordinate an escape plan. Once you are certain the area is reasonably stable, fix the victim's last seen point and mark the spot with a piece of equipment, such as a ski or pole. Turn your rescue beacon to receive and take the time to make sure everyone else does, too.

If you're not alone, the others in the party should quickly search the slide path for clues or signs of the victim. Although it seems obvious, be sure everyone is reminded to check gloves for a hand inside or for a foot in a boot still attached to a ski. All searchers should probe likely deposition areas after they have made their initial search. Anyone else in the group should come with you, moving slowly down the avalanche path, scuffing feet for shallowly buried clues and listening for the signal of the buried beacon. When someone picks up a signal, the rest of the group should continue their efforts. The person who picks up the signal should begin an organized beacon search. If there are enough rescuers, assign someone to get probes, shovels, and first-aid equipment ready.

WHAT TO DO IF SOMEONE ELSE IS CAUGHT IN AN AVALANCHE

- Watch the victim.
- Wait for the avalanche to stop.
- Make sure the area is safe to begin the rescue.
- Mark the victim's last seen spot.
- Turn your beacons to receive.
- Search for surface clues while you move down the slide path, listening for the signal.
- When you pick up the signal, begin a grid search.
- After probing to pinpoint the victim, get as many shovels going as you can to dig the person out.
- After digging the victim out, perform appropriate first aid.

THE GRID SEARCH METHOD

The traditional search pattern is a grid based on perpendicular lines crossing the points of maximum signal strength. The person who picks up the signal should orient her beacon for the strongest signal, then continue down the path listening for the signal to get

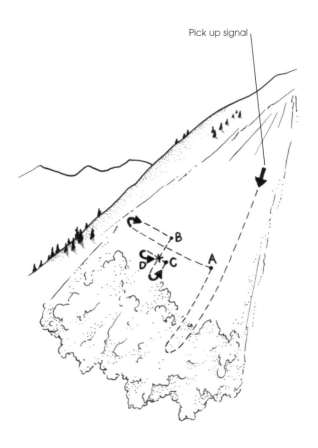

Figure 11. Grid search method

stronger (louder). Do not move the beacon when you have found the best orientation. The signal should transmit progressively stronger to a point and then start to get progressively weaker. Continue along the line until you are sure the signal is definitely becoming weaker, then return to the marked point of maximum volume, turning the volume control down until you can barely hear the signal (see figure 11).

Turn ninety degrees and begin the next pass. After a couple of steps, make sure the signal is getting stronger. If it is weaker or disappears, reverse your course. Again, mark the point where the signal is the strongest and continue on until the signal definitely fades. Return to the marked point, turn the volume down again until you can barely hear it, and repeat the process.

By this pass you should be close. Hold the beacon close to the snow and move in a direction perpendicular to the previous pass. The signal should get stronger quickly if you are going in the right direction. The volume control should be at its lowest setting, since the human ear is much more sensitive to changes in volume at lower volumes.

Once you have the volume control at the lowest setting, you are ready for the last series of passes. Get down on your knees and try to pinpoint the strongest signal by using a very limited-area grid pattern. You should narrow it down to an area no more than about

2 square feet as quickly as possible. At this point you will start probing for the exact location of the victim. Probing will be much more accurate and quicker, and will make shoveling efforts quicker and more efficient. The basic rule of probing is "Probe unto others as you would have them probe unto you." The victim wants you to find him, not skewer him.

TANGENTIAL SEARCH METHOD

Another method of beacon searching recently came into use and is known as the tangential or induction method. This method is based on intercepting the electromagnetic waves being transmitted by the buried unit. At the point of maximum signal strength in the first pass, you should stop, turn the volume down, and reorient the beacon. Theoretically, the strongest signal should be detected at a slight angle to your present direction of travel. By following this new direction, the signal strength should increase again. If it does not, go back to the position of the strongest signal and reorient your beacon (see figure 12).

At the point where the signal is strongest, stop and repeat the process. If you have a visual system of lights or digital distance readouts, this system will work even more efficiently. Eventually, this search method will take you on a series of slight tangent lines, creating an inward spiral leading to the buried victim. As

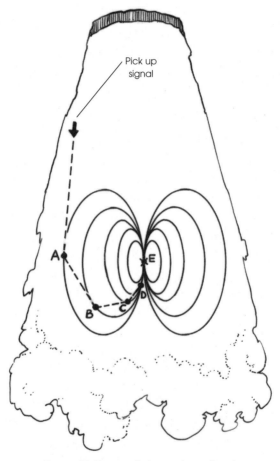

Pick up
signal

A

E

B

C

D

Figure 12. Tangential search method

you reach the point where the volume control is at its lowest setting, switch to the grid method and repeat the process as described in the previous section. The danger with this system is that by taking too great an angle, you may randomly walk along progressively shorter segments without any defined order. You will eventually find the victim, but it may take longer than the grid search method.

DIRECTIONAL SEARCH METHOD

The latest generation of beacons offers sophisticated antennas and computer-chip technology to allow what is finally a true "directional" search, i.e., the beacon tells you which direction to go to find the buried unit. This is obviously the most intuitive method, as it requires little more than paying attention and staying cool in a stressful situation. However, even these user-friendly units require practice and care to ensure the most efficient and effective search results.

RESCUING A BURIED VICTIM

The search should take less than five minutes. When you locate the victim, get as many shovels digging as possible; remember you need to uncover his head first. As soon as the victim's head is uncovered, check to see if he is breathing. If not, clear his airway and begin mouth-to-mouth resuscitation. It may take twenty or thirty minutes to dig him out if the debris is very deep or heavy—so keep monitoring him. Take care when pulling the person out, as he may have spinal or other life-threatening injuries. Once the victim is completely out, treat him for other injuries and hypothermia. See the FalconGuide *Wilderness First Aid*, by Gilbert Preston, MD, for information on dealing with wilderness medical emergencies.

Probe Search Techniques

If you cannot find a beacon signal after your initial search, try a second pass with the beacons and continue searching for surface clues. If no beacon signal is heard after a second pass, prepare for a hasty probe search. With your probes or ski poles, investigate likely deposition areas, particularly above rocks and around trees. The goal is to put as many holes in the snow as possible, increasing the chances of finding the victim in a short amount of time. If this still does not produce results, it is time to reorganize and perform a hasty probe search again.

Eventually, you may have to make a formal probe search if you still can't find the victim. At the toe of the slide, all the rescuers should stand elbow to elbow and probe at the toe of each of their feet, then move forward one foot and repeat the process. This is very time-consuming and fatiguing process, and the chances of making a live recovery are very slim at this point.

You may decide by this time to send for help if it is close by. Send two people if you can spare them. Before they leave, make sure you give them a note indicating the exact location of the slide and all other pertinent information. It is important to keep the safety and health of the rescuers in mind as well during the course of the rescue. The worst situation for the victim and rescuers is to have a subsequent slide.

Points to Ponder

Ultimately, we have little control over the natural forces that create avalanches, so we have to focus on the factor we can control—ourselves. Whether we place ourselves in harm's way or not depends on where we go, when we go, and how we travel. These decisions should be guided by a thorough understanding of how terrain, weather, and snowpack factors affect stability. As a result, it is possible to enjoy safe travel under even the most hazardous conditions.

Avalanches are a natural phenomenon, and we can do little to stop them. Therefore, we need to be able to assess when hazard exists, and then use good safe travel techniques to minimize the risks to our group and ourselves. The best strategy for safe travel through wilderness in winter is to use caution and make conservative decisions. When in doubt about a given slope, dig a pit and test the stability of the snowpack, or better yet, move to a lower angled slope, where the likelihood of a slide is much less. The surest way to avoid being caught in an avalanche is to avoid avalanche terrain completely.

If you decide to travel in avalanche terrain, make sure everyone in your party has a functioning avalanche transceiver (beacon), and each person knows how to use it. The use of beacons in a rescue situation is by far the fastest and most dependable way of finding a buried victim. Beacons should be switched to transmit at the beginning of the tour and left on during the entire tour. Be sure to replace the batteries regularly and check the transmitting and receiving distance. Each person should also have a sturdy shovel and probe poles.

Assess avalanche danger before entering avalanche terrain and update that opinion as you travel based on your field observations. Be constantly alert for clues about the stability of the snowpack. Look for signs of recent avalanches on neighboring slopes, and be sensitive to the sound and feel of the snow under your feet. Poke around in the snow and check the relative densities of buried layers. To learn more about the stability of the snowpack you may choose to dig a pit and conduct a shovel shear or Rutschblock Test.

Finally, make sure the group's objectives and alternative routes are understood, and everyone has a basic awareness of avalanche hazard and rescue techniques. Choose a leader and make a plan before you ever reach avalanche country.

Backcountry skiing and mountaineering can be safe and rewarding experiences if everyone accepts these responsibilities. Take an avalanche course with a field component. Read all you can about the subject and check out the excellent videos available. Armed with a basic awareness of avalanche hazard and common sense, we can all look forward to a lifetime of safe play in the winter wilderness environment.

Sources of Information

Organizations

American Association of Avalanche Professionals (AAAP)
Don Bachman (Executive Director), P.O. Box 1032,
Bozeman, MT 59771-1032

Books

Armstrong, Betsy and Knox Williams. *The Avalanche Book.* Golden, Colo.: Fulcrum, 1992.

Daffern, Tony. *Avalanche Safety for Skiers and Climbers.* Seattle: The Mountaineers, 1993.

Fessler, Doug and Jill Fredston. *Snow Sense.* Anchorage, Alaska: Mountain Safety Center, 1994.

La Chappelle, Edward. *The ABC's of Avalanche Safety.* Seattle: The Mountaineers, 1985.

McClung, David and Peter Schaere. *The Avalanche Handbook.* Seattle: The Mountaineers, 1993.

Preston, Gilbert, MD. *Wilderness First Aid.* Guilford, Conn.: The Globe Pequot Press, 1997.

Swedo, Suzanne. *Wilderness Survival.* Guilford, Conn.: The Globe Pequot Press, 1998.

Videos

Beating the Odds. The Canadian Avalanche Association, 1995.

Winning the Avalanche Game. The Utah Avalanche Forecast Center, 1993.

Avalanche Rescue Beacons. The Colorado Avalanche Information Center, 1996.

Web Sites

The Cyberspace Snow and Avalanche Center, www.csac.org

The Westside Avalanche Network (produced by the AAAP), www.avalanche.org

About the Author

John Moynier has lived in the High Sierra of California since 1978, working as a backcountry ski, snowboard, and climbing guide most of the time since. He is a certified ski-mountaineering guide with the American Mountain Guides Association (AMGA) and serves as a clinician/examiner for their ski-mountaineering program. He has guided throughout western North America, as well as in New Zealand and Australia.

John is also a freelance writer and photographer whose work has been published in numerous national magazines, including *Powder, Rock and Ice,* and *Backcountry.* He has also served as an editor for *Couloir* and *Cross Country Skier* magazines. He has authored a number of outdoors books, including *Backcountry Skiing in the High Sierra, Sierra Classics, Mammoth Area Rock Climbs,* and *Bishop Area Rock Climbs,* among others.